Trine L. Möller

GRANDMA DIES

Original Danish title: *Bedstemor dør*

Translated by Mary McGovern

Copyright © 2019 Trine L. Möller

Second edition 2020

Publisher: Books on Demand GmbH, Copenhagen, Denmark

Printer: Books on Demand GmbH, Norderstedt, Germany

ISBN 9788743015918

Hey Grandma!

I visit Grandma.

Grandma makes a kite with me.

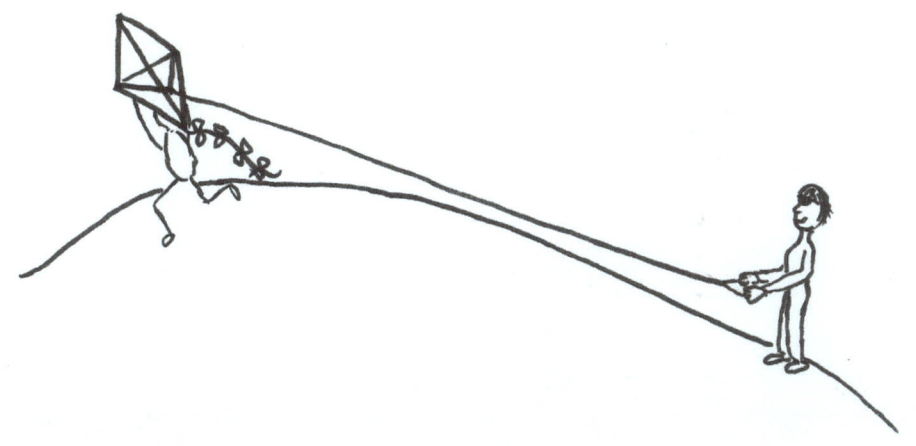

Grandma holds the string and I run with the kite.

I let go -

Wheeeeeeeeeeeeeeeeeeeeeeeeeeeee!

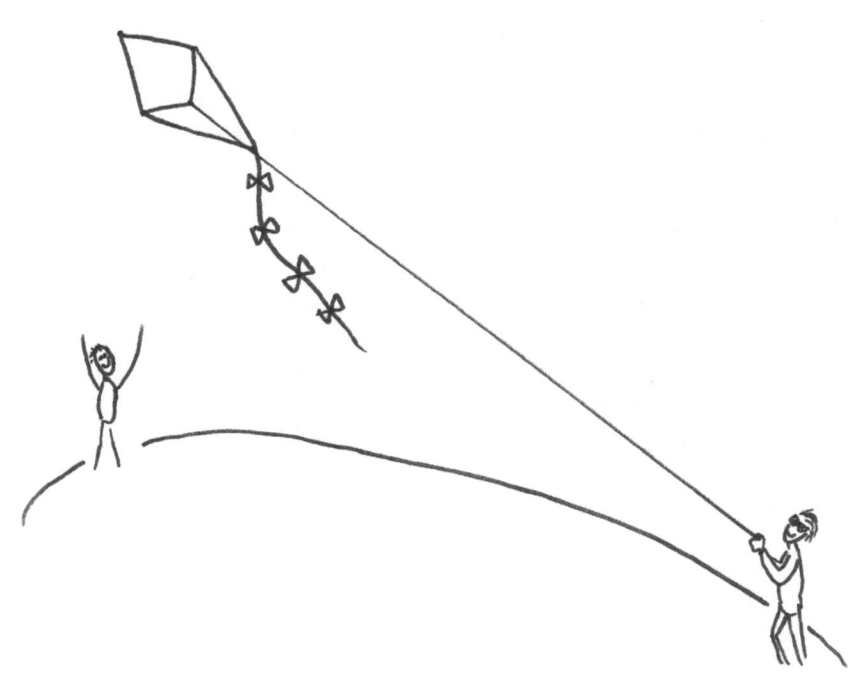

Grandma loves flying kites.

At Grandma's house we have a tea party with our cuddly toys.

Bye bye!

Cuddles the dog says goodbye to Mimi, Grandma's teddy.

Time passes.

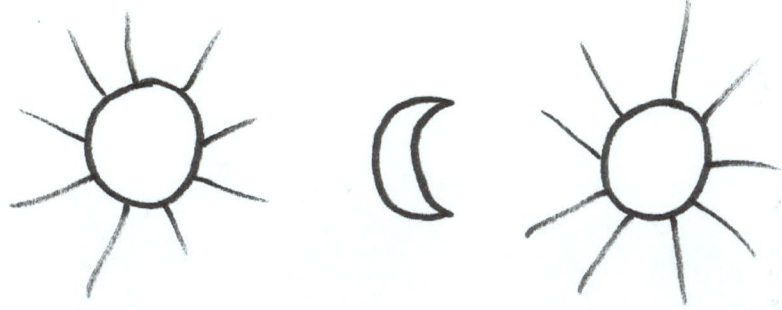

Grandma is dead.

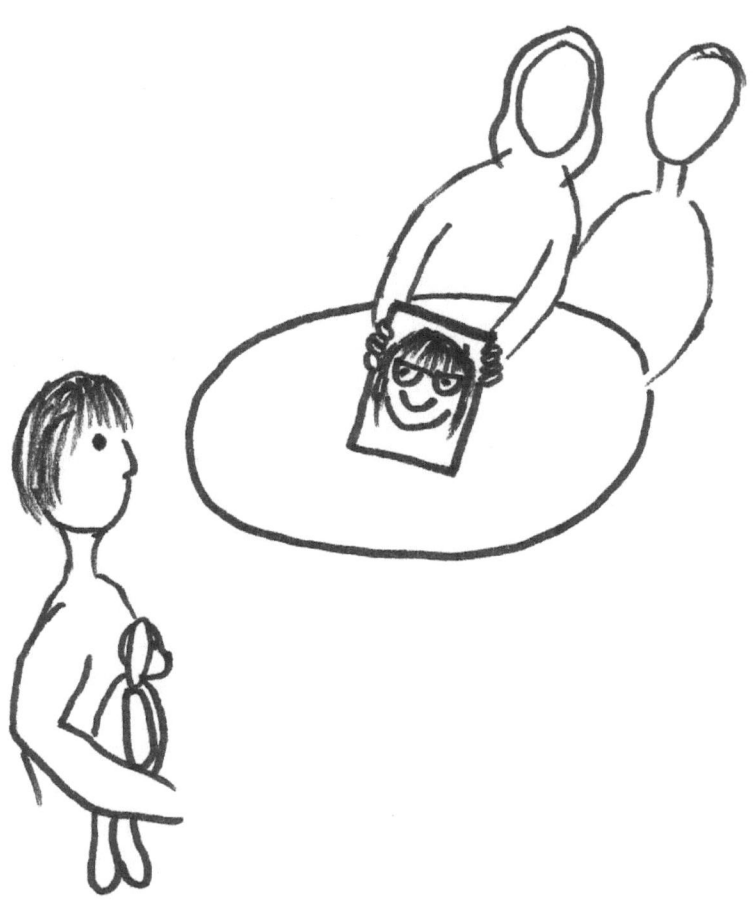

Mummy says that Grandma "passed away" in her sleep.

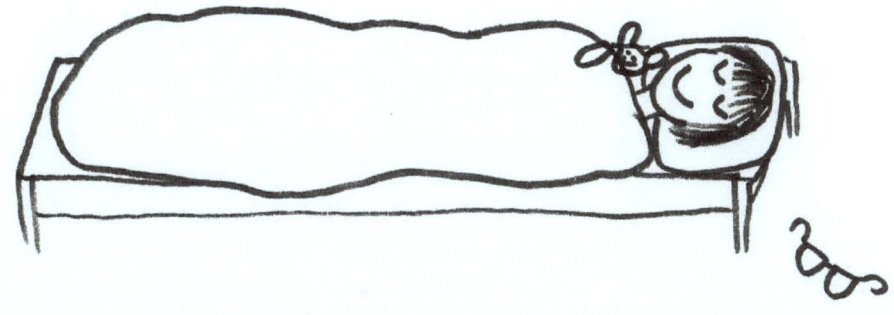

A blood vessel in Grandma's brain burst
while she was sleeping.
The blood flowed into her brain.
Then the brain couldn't make the body work
anymore.
Grandma stopped breathing and
her heart stopped beating.

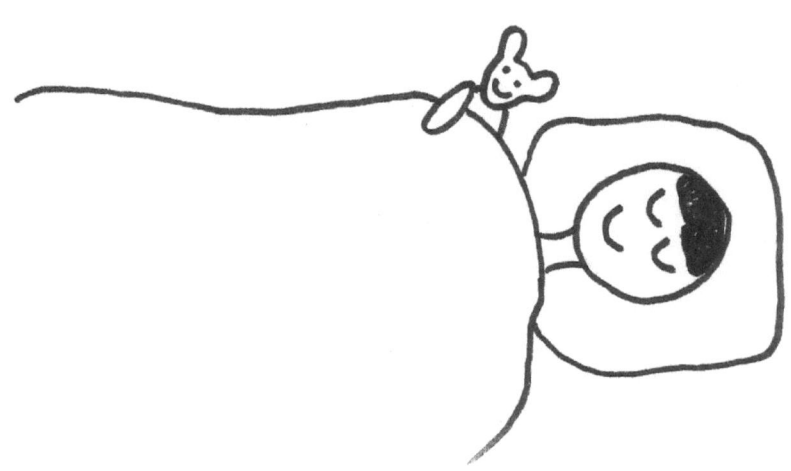

Grandma's spirit said goodbye
and thank you to her body.

Grandma's spirit is drawn towards the light.

Granddad and other loved ones who were already dead
welcome Grandma to the spiritual world.

At night when we are asleep, our spirit also visits the spiritual world. We just don't remember it.

In the spiritual world Grandma can make all the most
beautiful kites she wants.
She needs only to imagine them
and they appear.

After a long time in the spiritual world, people begin
to long for the physical world again.

They long to be able to chew a carrot, to feel the cold
and the snow – and the heat and the sunrays – and to
pat a dog and catch a ball.

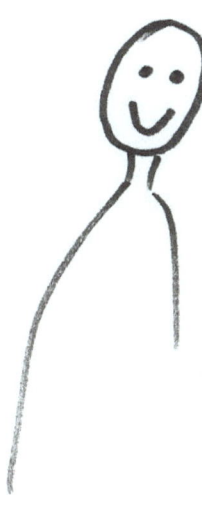

Now I am ready to be born again.

I just need a mother and father who suit me.

When the mummy and the daddy make a child,
the baby's spirit attaches itself to the new little body
growing in her tummy.

When the baby is born in the physical world
its spirit has forgotten all about the spiritual world,
just as you can't remember your short visits
in the spiritual world
while your body is resting during sleep every night.

The baby's spirit can't remember either
that she was Grandma's spirit a loooooooong time
ago.

The baby is now busy exploring the physical world
and learning to control her body,
so she can chew a carrot, pat a dog and throw a ball.

vuf

The book ends here
but the spirit lives on forever.